Personal Finance And Money Management

How To Get Out Of Debt, Save Money, And Start Investing For The Future

Phil C. Senior

Personal Finance And Money Management

Bluesource And Friends

This book is brought to you by Bluesource And Friends, a happy book publishing company.

Our motto is **"Happiness Within Pages"**

We promise to deliver amazing value to readers with our books.

We also appreciate honest book reviews from our readers.

Connect with us on our Facebook page www.facebook.com/bluesourceandfriends and stay tuned to our latest book promotions and free giveaways.

Don't forget to claim your FREE books!

Brain Teasers:
https://tinyurl.com/karenbrainteasers

Harry Potter Trivia:
https://tinyurl.com/wizardworldtrivia

Sherlock Puzzle Book (Volume 2)
https://tinyurl.com/Sherlockpuzzlebook2

Also check out our best seller book
"67 Lateral Thinking Puzzles"
https://tinyurl.com/thinkingandriddles

Personal Finance And Money Management

Table of Contents

Bluesource And Friends

Table of Contents

Description

Introduction

Chapter 1: Money Can Be Happiness

Chapter 2: Take Control of the Family Financials

    Keep Receipts

    Maintain a Diary

    Review the Receipts and Diary

    Reflect On Your Lifestyle

    Document Your Intentions

    Record Keeping

Chapter 3: Draft a Budget and Cut the Unnecessary Bleeding (Expenses)

    Design a Budget

Chapter 4: Build a Reserve but Don't Hoard It

    Engage In a Side Job

Personal Finance And Money Management

    Managing the Cash Reserve
    Considerations

Chapter 5: What Is the Difference Between Good Debt and Bad Debt? (Turn Your Credit Card into Good Debt and Not Bad Debt)

    Good Debt
    Illustrations of Good Debt
    Bad Debts
    Illustrations of Bad Debts
    How to Avoid Bad Debt
    Summary

Chapter 6: If You Have a Debt, Always Work Out a Repayment Plan

Chapter 7: Invest In Yourself (Financial Education Especially)

Chapter 8: Part-time Active & Passive Income Ideas (Tax Liens, Airbnb, Book or Audio Publishing, etc.)

    Uber and Other Taxi Applications
    Online Freelance Writing

Personal Finance And Money Management

Online/Digital Publishing

Coaching/Motivational Speaking/Mentoring

Airbnb

Transcription

Chapter 9: Get Insurance but Do Not Over Commit. Just Get the Basics that Will Cover Most of It

Car Insurance

House/Home

Health

Education

Chapter 10: Watch Out for Investing Scams

Specialized "Business"

Pyramid Schemes

Bubble Bursts

Suspicious Investors

Close Associates

Chapter 11: 401k Tips

Try to Diversify Assets

Personal Finance And Money Management

Maximize Employer's Matching Contribution

Aggressive Investment

Non-Revenue Sharing Fund Share

Low-Cost Investment

Retirement Account and 401k

Enhance Contributions

Critical Success Factors

Enhance Your Contributions to Grow Savings

Target Date Fund

Advantages of Using 401k Savings Account

Plan Advisor

Chapter 12: Hang Out with Like-Minded Friends Who are Conscious About their Financial Being

Conclusion

Personal Finance And Money Management

Description

What makes this book outstanding is its friendly approach to individuals who have never handled personal finance and money management, persons who have tried to make personal budgets and given up, and readers looking for a simple but pragmatic approach to personal finance management. These attributes are what separates this book from its peers. The author cautiously avoids overwhelming the reader with financial management jargon and theories, and instead guides the reader through self-awareness with respect to personal finances. The presentation by the author is simple but resourceful with a practical approach to designing a personal budget, defining and avoiding bad debt, making savings, and how to invest. The book gradually introduces you to techniques of learning to maintain a personal financial plan that will eventually graduate you into an investor.

Expectedly, the book packs critical areas of personal finance and money management, such as ways of taking control of family financials. The book further walks us through ways of drafting a budget and leaving out unnecessary expenses. The author covers planning for different money for different goals. As if not enough, the book walks us through ways of building a cash reserve but not hoarding, including defining for us what a good debt versus bad debt is. The author goes on to discuss how to repay a debt by having a repayment plan. The author then explores the ways in which you can invest in yourself. From these snapshots, this book combines content and delivery to make the reader competent and successful in personal finance and money management.

From the start, the book set to avoid too much fluff on personal finances, and the reader will find the content and its delivery devoid of burdensome theories and literature. The audience of this book is immediately immersed in ways of navigating out of bad debt to being an investor. The reader is not only knowledgeable but is also empowered to introduce others to personal finances management. The simple and friendly approach is meant to help demystify the issue of personal finances. The author explored ways of taking control of family financials. The book further guides the audience through ways of drafting a debt repayment plan, and lifestyle adjustments. The author introduces you to planning for different money for different goals and walked you through ways of building a cash reserve but not hoarding it.

It can then be concluded that this book offers a fresh and pragmatic approach to personal finance and money management. This book is appropriate for a reader who has tried personal finance management and given up several times, a reader new to personal finance management, and an individual that engages in personal budgeting but needs a systematic approach to enhance the positive outcomes.

We can conclude that if you are looking for a pragmatic approach to making a personal financial plan, managing debts, and making good personal investments, then this should be your choice. The book is written for native and international audiences by using a simple and jargon-free language. The layout of the chapters is systematic and connected, enabling the reader to develop knowledge and skills as you read through. The author has read a significant number of books and literature on the subject to enable the simplification of the content for all audiences, especially those aged 18 to 35 years. When writing this book, the author understood your needs.

Personal Finance And Money Management

Introduction

Congratulations on getting this book! In this book, I will walk you through managing your personal finances, avoiding bad debts, and making a meaningful investment. I have taken measures to make sure the language used is simple and that the tips given are pragmatic for an individual. The book is written with the assumption that you have never done personal finances, or if you did personal budgeting, it was for the sake of it and along the way you gave up on the tedious work needed to sustain it. For this reason, this book gradually gives you techniques of learning to keep a personal financial plan that will eventually graduate you to an investor. Let us now explore what each chapter carries for you.

Notably, Chapter 1 makes an argument that money is an enabler of happiness by allowing you to access the resources and services necessary to trigger happiness.

Personal Finance And Money Management

Chapter 1 acknowledges that money in itself is not happiness but it is an enabler of happiness when well managed. Chapter 2 explores ways of taking control of family financials. For Chapter 3, it guides you through ways of drafting a budget and leave out unnecessary expenses. Chapter 4 covers planning for different money for different goals. For Chapter 5, it walks you through ways of building a cash reserve but not hoarding. Chapter 6 dwells on what is a good debt versus bad debt. Chapter 7 discusses how to repay a debt by having a repayment plan. For Chapter 8, it explores ways in which you can invest in yourself. The chapter introduces some passive income ideas. Chapter 10 advises you to secure insurance but remember not to over commit. Chapter 11 cautions on investment scams. Chapter 12 gives 401k tips. Finally, Chapter 13 explores the need for the right circle of friends when pursuing personal financial management.

Chapter 1: Money Can Be Happiness

I know you have had conflicting statements and theories about the link of money and happiness or lack of happiness. We will take the argument that money can be a source of happiness. Money is a resource and not the happiness itself, and perhaps this is what creates confusion. Let us take a simple example of water. For all people, water is a resource and it depends on how we use water to get value out of it. For instance, one may use water for swimming, for laundry, for cleaning, and as a water fountain. Another person might decide to let the water run consuming everything in the house with wetness and, in this case, making water a great source of distress. The same is true with money; it all depends on an individual's discipline, goals, and management.

For one to survive, especially in the contemporary world, we need resources. We need services. For us to

Personal Finance And Money Management

feel comfortable, we need to have electricity, gas for our vehicles, water, and active health insurance. We cannot be happy if we are not comfortable first. While an individual may experience short-term happiness without all these resources, with time, the individual will have to look for a portion of these resources to induce happiness again. Additionally, we are now living in a formalized economy where the concept of a person being self-sufficient is fast waning. The implication of all these is that we cannot produce all that we need and this means we have to frequently source for some services and materials for our living.

Expectedly, this is where the criticality of money as an enabler to acquire resources surfaces. By having a requisite amount of money, we can acquire and pay for transport, electricity, and water. With an adequate amount of money, we can access high-quality healthcare and fix our aching bodies. Money is necessary for one to acquire needed resources as mentioned. However, since money is a resource, it means that its supply is limited and we must have a way of ensuring that we spend this resource prudently. Just like any other resource, like oil, we need to consistently monitor and manage acquisition, usage, and saving money for the future.

If there are a plan and financial management then the link between money and happiness will exist. By having a good personal budget or family budget, a family will conveniently afford primary needs such as education, healthcare, food, and clothing. The family may also afford holidays and other recreational needs. It can then be argued that when family stresses and worries are minimized or eliminated, then the family will have adequate time to explore other critical areas of life. As an illustration, a couple will spend quality time at home discussing the progress and future of their children, devoid of incessant complaints and emotional breakdowns. By having time and resources to focus on children, the children may be cautioned

Personal Finance And Money Management

against poor parenting outcomes such as experimenting with alcoholism. All these illustrations suggest that the link between money and happiness exist but conditionally.

While they are numerous inputs to attain happiness, affordability, and acquisition of basic resources is necessary for achieving happiness. It is not possible for one to be happy when you cannot afford house rent, cannot pay for electricity, and cannot occasionally afford a simple holiday. The argument here is that money is not happiness but money is the greatest enabler of happiness. Therefore, with a good financial plan that allows balancing of social life and work life or business life, a person has a significant opportunity to not only be happy but also create happiness for those around him or her.

Finally, money, as a potential source of happiness, is the reward phenomenon of earning or making money. When one accomplishes his or her individual targets at work or in business, money is a common and acknowledged reward. When a person improves the management of his personal finances, the result is making more savings, which is a great source of feeling not only happiness but also feeling invaluable. We can summarize the attributes of having money that qualify it as an inducer of happiness as being an enabler of acquiring resources, services, and commodities; as a reward for an individual's efforts and creating a path to move into a comfort zone.

Summary

As argued, the link between happiness and money exists, but conditionally. The requisite condition for triggering happiness arising from making and having money is personal financial management. It is while preparing a financial plan that one can further add a social philosophy to money to humanize it. Well-managed money will enable one to afford material resources needed to make life comfortable and help create room for other social and familial engagement that can elicit happiness. The truth is that significant time is spent sourcing money or repaying the money at the expense of the family. Extended work can harm the personal connection between family members. In this manner, having a personal budget equals addressing one of the root causes of familial disputes and disconnections.

Chapter 2: Take Control of the Family Financials

Keep Receipts

Before we move to the specifics of how to manage family financials, it is important to first understand what the sources of this information are. It is important that you keep grocery store receipts and where you use electronic money such as Visa Card, and make sure you get the financial statement of your weekly or monthly spending. You can print, write, or store these proofs of expenditure. The mistakes people make when it comes to managing their finances, is to force a financial plan on their lives which leads to abandoning of the good initiative. By gathering proofs of your monthly expenditure, you are getting ready for a data-driven approach. In other terms, you should design your financial plan based on your lifestyle.

Maintain a Diary

It is recommended that you get a personal diary dedicated to capturing finance-related thoughts and targets. In this diary, have a column for expected injections of income. Again, have another column for expected expenditure. Lastly, have a column for miscellaneous expenditure. Now, each time you spend anything to try to capture it under either the listed expenditure, miscellaneous expenditure, or each time you make money, also capture it under the expected income. The mistake most people trying to control their finances make is to impose financial control in themselves instead of developing it. In this segment, we are trying to get the true picture of our financial inflows and outflows as opposed to making assumptions.

Review the Receipts and Diary

Making a review of your expenditure is necessary but it should align with your lifestyle. As argued earlier, imposing a financial plan on yourself will fail as you will prioritize yourself over everything else. The qualification of requiring you to keep and then review receipts is to help you define your lifestyle in terms of finances and then make a projection out of it. The primary intent of this exercise is to gauge if you are living beyond your means by calculating the percentage of total expenses against income. If the expenses equal or exceed the income, then you are living beyond your means and are highly vulnerable to the slightest financial shocks such as salary delay.

Reflect On Your Lifestyle

Now that you have gotten a picture of how your finances look, the next step is to do some reflection. Before you start your reflection, have a writing pad or notebook with you. Try to think again and again of things that you can do without in the short-term and long-term. Again, think over the things that you have to do with but can revise their consumption downward; for instance, expenditure on television and soft drinks. Think of other ways of making simple saves such as switching off lights that are not in use. Think of slight discomfort that can have a high impact, such as adjusting the hot shower to lukewarm, which can lead to significant energy consumption save.

Document Your Intentions

It is now time to match the intentions against the financial inflows and outflows. Make a mock new financial plan with the saving intention. For instance, make electricity expense to be 10% less if it is part of items that can be improved to realize savings. Leave out items that you can do without with little adverse impact on your life such as junk food. Lastly, include the non-financial intention of wanting to have a personal budget such as more family time.

Record Keeping

One of the most ignored aspects of managing personal finances is record-keeping. Without good record keeping, the whole endeavor will not succeed. It is important to purchase a file, a paper punch, and have a safe but easily accessible place to keep the finances. If you have a family, make sure to involve them and let them know why they should bring back receipts of purchase or any other proof of purchase or expenditure. In case you are using a computer to do the entire endeavor, then it is important to have a home computer and a separate account for maintaining records on personal finances.

Chapter 3: Draft a Budget and Cut the Unnecessary Bleeding (Expenses)

Design a Budget

At this point, we have all the necessary data, information, and understanding for making a personal budget. Expenses will include water bill, gas bill, electricity bill, school fees, and insurance fees among other items. Then, there is always a chance of unexpected expenditure that cannot be avoided. All this will be captured under the expenses column. Using previous data and information we created in Chapter 2, we will now make estimations or projections. This is what budgeting is all about. While we have a provision for unexpected but necessary expenses, they should be minimized. You should try hard to only spend on identified areas and this is the

Personal Finance And Money Management

hallmark of financial discipline. Remember that it is not pleasurable to cut expenses because it might imply less comfort, but it will pay in the long run.

The candidate areas for cutting expenditures include spending money on lottery tickets or gambling. Money spent on entertainment, especially nightclubs and beers, can also be significantly reduced. The money spent on soft drinks can be significantly reduced. The other areas for cutting expenses include telephone bills. Where necessary, use texting and instant messaging such as WhatsApp that can consume less credit. Instead of the individual phone getting its data, you can install home Wi-Fi that can be shared by everyone. Remember, the most bothersome expenses are the recurrent expenses.

Another way of reducing expenses is to shop around for stores that occasionally offer discounts. There are good stores that give discounts and you should prefer them over the status quo. Sometimes, buying in bulk

Personal Finance And Money Management

will cost less than buying several smaller units of the same product. For this reason, take time to determine the best way to purchase by selecting stores, smaller or larger units, and any discounts offered. Family shopping contributes significantly to monthly expenses, and managing it will reflect positively in the evaluation of your budget. Having active health insurance is critical to avoid unexpected health expenses.

Concerning assets, let the acquisition of assets be long-term. You should phase the purchase of electronics, furniture, cars, and any other asset over a considerable period of time. Individuals frequently purchase new phones, DVD player, and cameras. While it might be difficult to avoid the temptation to upgrade your electronics, make sure it is done over a considerable period of time. If kept well, a mobile phone can serve you for several years before requiring a replacement. If possible, have a disposal plan that can generate some cash from your assets, especially electronics that become obsolete much faster as well as depreciating fast compared to other forms of assets.

Remarks

A common mistake that most individuals make is to punish themselves rather than cut expenses. It is important to understand that cutting your budget means denying yourself some comforts. For this reason, you should begin with either significantly revising down your expenses while keeping all the items in the budget, or cutting out only a few and then gradually widening the cuts. The human body, in particular, tends to adjust gradually to changes and you should not let your mind and excitement rush you. These suggestions are anchored in a multi-discipline understanding of human behavior, especially psychology.

Chapter 4: Build a Reserve but Don't Hoard It

Now that we have a budget that is guiding you and you have revised it to make sure that expenses do not gobble more than 50% of your income, you should now create a savings account. Take measures to ensure that the saving account is not linked to your credit cards or phone applications to minimize the temptation of withdrawing money from the account. By saving in this account each month, you are building a financial reserve. The cash reserve should be built based on the saving goals you set. You should maintain high discipline and avoid the temptation to use some of this cash and reimburse later. Not making any withdrawal from this account should be part of your goals or objectives.

Personal Finance And Money Management

Apart from savings made, any other money you make should be kept in this account. For instance, monetary rewards, a pay rise, or bonus payments constitute unplanned income and should be saved. When given a shopping voucher, you should save a similar amount in your bank's savings account. Even with an unexpected financial boost, you should always stick to your personal budget, which is managing expenses and saving as much as possible with acceptable levels of comfort. When you purchase goods on a discount, remember to save that money and you should not spend the discounted amount on more shopping.

After three months, you will notice your savings account is growing and you might be adjusting to the foregone comforts. It is important to acknowledge that you will feel the temptation to immediately invest the cash saved. It is not yet advisable to immerse yourself in investments even though there might be alluring offers in the market. The focus should remain saving and building cash reserves. The motivations for saving and building cash reserves include the assurance that, in case of a pay freeze or loss of a job, you can still manage your monthly expenses. The greatest threat to building a cash reserve is the failure to stick to a budget, as well as making a withdrawal from the savings account.

Engage In a Side Job

If your schedule allows, another effective way to build a cash reserve is to engage in a side job. For instance, they are numerous opportunities online that one can work to generate income. The income generated should be saved. Avoid the temptation to use this extra income to sustain the previous lifestyle. Any money made from side jobs should be saved. While engaging in side jobs, take measures to align with your personal budget. A side job should not eat into your budget and it should not exhaust you. Other side jobs that are not online can include training a local club or giving motivational talks.

Managing the Cash Reserve

Now that you have explored ways of enhancing the cash reserve, take time to design ways of setting conditions for access and use of the cash reserve. For instance, one of the conditions can be that the cash reserve can only be accessed during emergencies, such as a delay in salary payment or a health emergency. The conditions for access can include only one emergency access per month. The withdrawn amount should not be more than a third of the total saved amount. Additionally, you can also have a home saving kit where you deposit coins and notes and break it to bank them.

Considerations

One of the aspects of personal finance that most individuals overlook concerns donations to charities and extended family support. Even does not engage in such activities, it is important to plan and budget for them. In case one does not spend on any of these activities, then the money should be transferred to the savings accounts. The importance of planning for donations to charities as well as extended family support is to minimize items placed under the miscellaneous expenditure.

Lastly, after two years, you can start exploring good investment plans. If you are uncertain of engaging in investments that are low risk, then you can leave the cash in the savings account. However, you should consider making a low-risk investment to generate more income. When you make an investment, remember that the returns are the profit and this is what you can use to adjust your financial spending. After a period of time, you will feel the need to adjust your budget upward. The rule is to make sure you are living with your means by using the stated formula of "Living beyond your means=Expenses/Income." If the ratio or percentage is low, all the better. A high ratio or percentage, in this case, means that your expense is more than your income and this is a red flag. You should remember that financial discipline, like any office discipline or school discipline, will take away some of your pleasures but it is worth the try.

Summary

In practice, it is easier to save money but difficult to build a cash reserve. The reason for this flaw is, maintaining the discipline of not withdrawing or using part of the cash reserve is a challenge to most people. It is for this reason that the author suggests you make it difficult to access the bank account where you are building a cash reserve. For instance, the author suggests that you avoid linking the cash reserve bank account with phone withdrawal access or automated teller machine card access. For a start, the author thinks that it will be beneficial to avoid quick access to withdrawing or using the saved cash until you learn financial discipline. Think of a cash reserve as having a fridge full of various foodstuffs, but you have to

Personal Finance And Money Management

wait till the agreed time to eat because you are trying to avoid adding weight.

Chapter 5: What Is the Difference Between Good Debt and Bad Debt? (Turn Your Credit Card into Good Debt and Not Bad Debt)

Good Debt

A debt is considered good if it is a reasonable investment in an individual's financial future. Good debt is the one that helps generate income or leads to the target asset appreciating in value. For this reason, a good debt requires one to have elaborate reasons for wanting to borrow, where to borrow, and the terms of borrowing. Emphasis should be placed on how much you intend to borrow and the repayment plan against the needed adjustments you will make in your lifestyle. It might be necessary to consult beyond your friend circle on where to get an affordable loan and what the national economic projections imply. A good practice with taking a loan is that it should be accompanied by a downward lifestyle adjustment.

Illustrations of Good Debt

An example of good debt is borrowing money to invest in real estate after carefully reviewing the industry's information and projections. Real estate tends to have significant returns when the right investment portfolios are chosen. If you took a loan to invest in real estate, then you are likely to generate income that will help service the debt. When the investment helps repay part, or all of, entire loan, then the debt is not a dead-weight debt. One should avoid the temptation to borrow to the maximum allowable amount and only borrow what is absolutely necessary, because debt can be a risk to your entire investment and credit profile.

In addition to the examples above, borrowing money to invest in your business is good debt. A loan to enable you to grow your business constitutes good borrowing subject to the existence of a reasonable and realistic business model. Should the business pick up, then it will generate profits as well as appreciating its value, all of which can make servicing the loan easier. Purchasing a car that you can afford can be qualified as a good borrowing case as a car is critical to get you to work and earn your living. It is, however, important to take into account the costs of running the car against your income.

Bad Debts

The debts that drain your finances and wealth have no real prospect of servicing themselves and are not affordable, constitute bad debts. Unlike good debts, bad debts tend to have no realistic servicing plans and arise when individuals make impulse buying of items. Taking a loan to pay recurrent expenditure such as water bills, rent, and electricity bills constitute a bad debt. When one does cannot afford to secure a loan but manages to get a loan, then this is an example of bad debt. With bad debt, one will find it a challenge to make regular and affordable repayments.

Illustrations of Bad Debts

An illustration of bad borrowing may include securing a loan to go on a luxury holiday that you cannot afford. If a luxury holiday is accompanied by long-term debt, then it should be avoided. It is advised that you make savings first instead of getting into debt and restructure your plans to enable you to take a holiday or an affordable vacation. Making a purchase of a brand-new car that you cannot afford or need on a loan is bad debt. New cars depreciate, and should you lose your job, then you will sell the car at lesser amounts than you paid. As mentioned earlier, taking a loan to pay bills is an example of bad debt.

How to Avoid Bad Debt

There are several ways to avoid bad debt. First, shop around for the best deal. Interrogate yourself if you are borrowing the money cheaply as it can get. Ask yourself if you will manage to cope with an interest rise in the future. Then ask yourself if you will afford the monthly repayments comfortably. Again, ask yourself if borrowing the money will translate to improve financial status in the long-term. Now, ask yourself if you comprehend the risks involved should things go completely wrong. Lastly, question yourself if you understand the terms and conditions linked to securing this loan. Finally, establish the amount of money you need to borrow and understand that securing a loan amount of more than what you need will convert a good debt into bad debt.

Summary

In brief, good debt is the one that generates some income to help service the outstanding amount. In this manner, good debt will have a minimal negative impact on an individual's financial status. The intentions for seeking a good debt are clear and measurable. It is important to plan for servicing the debt by engaging in lifestyle adjustments if necessary. The other aspect of a good debt requires you to scout for affordable credit. Affordability is both financial and non-financial. The time required to service a good debt is reasonable with respect to your financial status and the risk of losing your investment should be minimal.

A cardinal rule for what is good debt is that it should not be used to settle recurrent expenditure such as electricity bills or cable TV bills. However, some utilities can become a good debt or bad debt depending on how you exploit the utility. For instance, using a credit card to pay for the Internet and then using Internet access to do an online job qualifies as good debt. On the other hand, using the same Internet purely for non-financial purposes such as social media may be regarded as bad debt. The emphasis here is that, sometimes, bad or good debt may be conditional, especially with technology services such as the Internet.

Chapter 6: If You Have a Debt, Always Work Out a Repayment Plan

In Chapter 5, we covered what constitutes a good debt and a bad debt. However, even with good debt, a poor repayment plan midway will convert a good debt into bad debt. The first thing you need to do is to develop a workable repayment plan. It is important that you avoid the temptation to make lump sum payment if your budget does not accommodate such flexibility. Once you have developed a repayment, make sure to align with the terms and conditions given for the loan secured. In case you have several debts, you might want to schedule their repayments on one day or pace them as per what works out for you. It is important to have a single view of all of your financial obligations including loan repayments.

The next step involves making repayments. If possible, your repayments should be more than the required minimum amounts. Loan repayments should be captured under your expenses column in your personal budget. Another way of ensuring that your loan repayments are timely is to have a separate bank account with a standing order. A standing order is an instruction to your bank to be making automatic deductions and transferring them to the specified account at a specified date for the defined period. Should you choose this route, it is important to ensure that the account with the standing order has an adequate amount to avoid overdraft charges that constitute another debt.

Third, as suggested, consider harmonizing all your loan repayments. Some people will prefer having all loan repayments on the same date while others will prefer spacing the loan repayments. What is important is for you to acknowledge the total loan repayments due and capture these as expenses within your monthly budget. It is important to avoid the temptation of the refinancing of loans as it only encourages you to engage in unplanned loans. You should take time to check if your bank actually implements the standing order in case you prefer servicing the loans through standing orders. By having all your loans harmonized, you will get the cost of repayments per month and plan accordingly.

Furthermore, it is necessary to make a few sacrifices when servicing a loan. You should understand that taking a good debt is still a cost in the short-term and sacrifices are needed to ensure that you maintain your financial status at desirable levels. Assuming that the entire loan was not used on the intended project or investment, the remaining amount should be used to repay the loan immediately. With loans that have a long grace period, you should assume that you are required to service the loan immediately and start making mock deductions that you save in the account that will be used to pay the loan. By doing this, when the time for paying the loan starts, repayment will not only be manageable but you can make a lump sum repayment, which buys more time and flexibility to grow the investment that is required in the loan in the first place.

Correspondingly, it is important to adjust your lifestyle expenses to acknowledge and accommodate loan repayment needs. For instance, you can sign up for Uber to occasionally benefit from offering limited taxi services when free. You should lessen your frequency of engaging in entertainment such as drinking, subscribing for several cable TV providers, and unnecessary upgrades of electronics when servicing a loan. It is almost impossible to avoid taking a loan, and while this is true, the managing loan repayments are critical to reducing the risk of the loan. Remember that credit can be an asset and a risk; it all depends on your plan and financial discipline.

Chapter 7: Invest In Yourself (Financial Education Especially)

Like any management issue, personal finance management requires certain skills and improvement of current skills. There are numerous open source online learning sites that make it easy to understand and apply personal financial management skills. One of the sites is www.incharge.org. When taking a financial literacy course, it is important to remember that your aim is to improve your personal financial skills rather than completing the entire course. You should not burden yourself to acquire all knowledge and skills presented at the particular site. The online financial literacy sites are comprehensive and you should take one topic at a time. For consistency, I suggest that you pick only one site and go through the lessons.

Personal Finance And Money Management

One of the areas you need education and exploration is budgeting and saving. The foundation of your financial plan is a good budget and commitment to savings. Through personal financial literacy that is offered online, you will explore how to minimize expenses, budget, and specify saving goals among others. Remember to challenge yourself to improve the efficiency of each category in your personal budget. The primary focus of a personal budget should remind reducing expenses and increasing the emergency fund. The other areas that you should learn include ways of budgeting, how to compute debt-to-personal income ratio, as well as how to grow your cash reserves.

Additionally, areas covered in financial literacy include how to understand your credit report and saving money at stores. Most individuals may not fully comprehend how a credit score is computed and what the credit report implies. You will also need to understand how to improve your credit report as well as making sure that a credit report accurately reflects you. A good credit score may enable you to secure a loan with favorable terms. With that loan and having literacy in the budget-making, you should then start your path from debt faster. A budget can also be considered as a ledger capturing the spending decisions that one intends to make.

Equally important, you should take a financial literacy class that addresses saving and investment. Most people assume a lot when it comes to savings and investment, and end up making no savings or no investments at all. Without literacy on savings and investments, you are also at risk of making unfruitful investments. For instance, it is important to save and invest for retirement while working. While most people agree that a comfortable retirement life does not happen overnight, few individuals actually commit to investing in life after retirement. From this illustration, it is necessary for one to seek expert opinion on how to approach the important issue of savings and investment.

Another area of personal finance that requires financial literacy is budgeting for a baby. For instance, when budgeting for a baby, you should consider diapers, baby formula, and loss of income. For instance, you can bring down the cost of diapers by alternating cloth and diapers, but you should take into consideration the comfort and health of the baby. You can also explore diaper services within your locality if you do not wish to clean them yourself. On formula milk, you should consider breastfeeding to lower the cost of formula milk. There are also beneficial gains from breastfeeding such as passing on natural immunities.

There is also an area that affects personal finances that individuals need to be taken through by experts on how to navigate it and this concerns loss of income. Assuming that one is employed, it is important to anticipate that the loss of a job can occur and devise remedial measures to minimize this risk. For instance, loss of a job can be minimized by professional career growth as well as engaging professional networking to ensure that one's attractiveness to the labor market is high. The other way of lessening the risk of job loss is to engage in small business investments with significant incomes. In case you are married, you should encourage and ensure that your partner is also engaged in an income-generating activity to ensure that, in case of a snap job loss, the other partner can support the family for a limited period.

Chapter 8: Part-time Active & Passive Income Ideas (Tax Liens, Airbnb, Book or Audio Publishing, etc.)

Uber and Other Taxi Applications

Making money, in addition to your salary income, is critical for you to realize meaningful savings plans as well as realize a significant reduction in your debt obligations. If you have a car, you can register it with Uber or any other carpooling app to enable you to occasionally engage in side income generation. During weekends, you can engage in Uber taxi service and earn some income. You can also use your car as a carpool and make some income as you leave for a job. All these side engagements are welcome, as long as they do not make you strain or affect your main source of income activity such as a job.

Online Freelance Writing

There are numerous sites that require editors, proofreaders, and freelance writers for articles for a website or newspaper. The cost of resources needed to work online is minimal, and in most cases, they only include an Internet connection, a laptop, and a smartphone. For just two hours to three hours a day, you can make fifty dollars a day and this can help generate significant income at home. Most company websites require a frequent update of their content, and they often outsource that task, which you can do and earn some income. There is also online data entry that pays attractively and can be done anywhere, especially at home. The advantage of online work is that it can inadvertently help you become more knowledgeable, thus offering double gains: knowledge and money.

Online/Digital Publishing

Closely related to freelance writing online, you can also do e-books on several topics. The topics are simple enough and adequate content is already online, enabling you to quickly immerse in writing e-books. Individuals are looking for books that offer practical guidelines for healthy eating, exercising, and staying married. These are topics that you can explore and write an e-book that is sold online through platforms such as e-Bay and Kindle. The good thing is that most companies that outsource writing also provide guidelines and tutorials on how to write your first book. There is also specialized software that can help format and check the content to qualify it for publishing.

Coaching/Motivational Speaking/Mentoring

Outside the online world, you can also engage in coaching volleyball, football, or hockey among other sports in your locality. If you are talented, knowledgeable, and skilled in a particular sport, you can offer yourself as an assistant trainer with any of the local clubs and associations near your locality at a fee. You can also do motivational speaking to school children or youths in your area at a small fee. If you have the qualification and reputation, you can offer yourself for motivational speaking that targets the youth or your group of interest in the community. There are a lot of opportunities to engage in that can generate you some income apart from your main job.

Airbnb

Assuming that you have a house, but you are sometimes required to travel for several weeks far away, then you can also list your house on Airbnb to temporarily rent it out to guests. The Airbnb offers a platform to temporarily make your house a guest house and earn some income rather than keeping it idle. Like any hotelier business, make sure to generate interest from prospective guests who may want to book in your listed house. Invest in making your house listing visible to potential guests. It is also important to update your calendar listing on Airbnb to ensure that it is offering more accurate information.

Transcription

It is one of the online work opportunities where you can also engage in transcribing content at a fee. They are even greater opportunities for other foreign languages where individuals require audio content to be transcribed and then translated to another language. Like the other online jobs, transcription work requires a computer, an Internet connection, and a smartphone. Transcription work can generate a significant income by just working two hours to four hours at home. All these passive and active income generation activities are meant to generate extra earning that can be used to enhance the move toward a smaller debt financial status.

Chapter 9: Get Insurance but Do Not Over Commit. Just Get the Basics that Will Cover Most of It

Having insurance provides peace of mind against the unseen. Disasters of different nature and magnitude can reverse your gains and set you on the path of bankruptcy. It is important to identify assets or aspects of your life that need insurance. The common candidate areas for insurance include car, education, house, and health. If you have a business, you will also need to find different categories of insurance such as fire, theft, and natural disasters. Insurance is vital as it will help restore your status quo in case of a disaster such as a hurricane battering your home, sweeping your car, or vandalism of your property. While insurance is great, you should take care not to overdo it.

Personal Finance And Money Management

Car Insurance

For a car, make sure you go for a full insurance package that covers against accidents, vandalism, theft, and damage by hurricane among other aspects. Since you will use the car to move pretty much everywhere, the risks to the car will also increase and it is of benefit to ensure that the car is covered against most risks to avoid taking you back to the start. Unlike other assets, comprehensive car insurance is beneficial to the owner because of the likelihood of any of the risks insured against happening. There is little downsizing that one can do when it comes to insuring a car, especially a personal car.

House/Home

You should insure your home against fire, floods, and vandalism. These three risks, when they occur, will render you in a precarious position, financially and emotionally. Fire at home can arise from negligence, arson, and electrical faults. Fire can also occur due to the fire spreading from a neighbor's house. Hazards such as hurricanes have been known to destroy houses and everything in the house, rendering families not just homeless but also hopeless. The frequency of occurrence of hurricanes is relatively high. Vandalism can arise from criminal elements or an unruly street demonstration, especially if your house is along a road that is commonly used by different groups of protestors.

It is important to avoid overdoing insurance even though securing your home against all imaginable threats is welcome. For instance, there is no need to secure your home against damage by freezing weather or damage to electronics due to a power surge. Now, all these aspects are a concern but if you are trying to get out of debt, then you can do without them in the short-term. There are insurance firms that can cover against damage of a house from animals and insects. However, for a person trying to improve his or her cash reserves, this overdoing of insurance cover is not necessary.

Health

Health cover is critical because health is everything, and one cannot precisely predict when you will fall sick or what will afflict you. Health conditions are a big threat to your personal budget as they can drain everything. Take time to perform a family history of chronic diseases and go for a health cover that is likely to ease your health costs now and in the future. However, take caution not to overdo it, such as insuring against loss of hair and any other aspects of health that can be foregone to spare more money for building cash reserves.

Education

Having an educational plan is important. Part of preparations for a baby is to have an education cover, where you save to ensure that school fees are assured and will not dent your personal budget. It is important to go for an insurance plan that does not take much of your monthly income, while still giving you acceptable for education cover. You can start with primary education to high school education coverage to allow you some leverage in your budget. Taking an education is a good investment in as much it is an expense. In all, insurance is important but the objective here is to find a way to free yourself from overdoing it, and instead, seize this opportunity to build your cash reserves.

Chapter 10: Watch Out for Investing Scams

Specialized "Business"

Due to the immense possibilities occasioned by technology and access to information, one is likely to fall for investment scams while thinking it is a genuine high-return business. While Bitcoin is not an outright scam, it is a cryptocurrency; it requires certain knowledge and skills to benefit from it. Another genuine business that requires specialized knowledge and skills includes forex trading. With these two illustrations, do not fall for the temptations to sink your hard-earned money with the promise of earning thousands to millions. These are high-return ventures, but they require a highly specialized and dedicated person to navigate the high risks associated with them. The problem is compounded by unscrupulous individuals or companies that market these high-risk ventures or quick-get-rich schemes as things that anyone can invest in.

Pyramid Schemes

A simple definition of a pyramid scheme is a deceitful con scheme which is presented as a genuine business, where members are encouraged to recruit others and the early members get to recover their investments while the latter members lose all. The business structure and operations of a pyramid scheme are designed to be shady to make it difficult to trace and recover the cash. Most pyramids are alluring as an initial member will have proof of high returns within a short time, and you might be tempted to believe the individual. For any investment, take time to ensure that the business is legitimately registered, and the terms and conditions provide a middle ground between you and the business.

Bubble Bursts

There are also genuine business and legitimate business ideas that can assume a scam-like dimension. For instance, if the media airs a story that there is a high demand for dogs as pets and thousands of people venture into dog breeding and selling dogs, then if you go ahead and join the business, it might become too risky. If you engage in such a business without due market research, then you might encounter a glut, or the market will simply fail to create demand anymore. Conducting market research and feasibility of a product is critical should you intend to invest in such ideas.

Suspicious Investors

There are also investment companies whose investment portfolio is questionable. Take time to go through a choice investment company to make sure that your funds are well-protected in case a company investment backfires. There are unscrupulous companies that write their terms and conditions or promise to generate high returns from select investments, when they know they are not genuine in this claim. Such companies invest in convincing advertisements, gather funds from the public, and generate minimal to zero income for investors, but are protected by the terms and conditions. With this in mind, it is important to review the history of an investment company and review its terms and conditions for a particular investment package.

Close Associates

Your close associates, with full knowledge that you have a significant cash reserve, may convince you to invest in their ideas or businesses with a promise of significant returns. If such an individual has a wicked intention, they will remit 'profits' for the first few months to entice you to commit more funds, then go ahead to report a loss or closure. As with the other segments, your money should only flow into a well-thought and protected investment, both at personal and third-party levels. The golden rule is to acknowledge that you and your money are different entities held together by respect and good intent.

It is important to always detect investment scams, as high-return investments require certain risks. Additionally, due to technology, there are new high return forms of business. It can become very difficult to ascertain how genuine a new business is, because technology is causing disruptions in the market and authorities are playing a catch-up game. However, by reviewing the terms and conditions given, one can gauge if his or her funds are secured or unsecured. An investment that secures your funds will go into extra length to generate profits and minimize all forms of risks.

Chapter 11: 401k Tips

Try to Diversify Assets

Like any other investment, ensure you diversify your 401k investments. Diversification can be achieved by selecting funds from different classes of assets, such as international stocks, local stocks, and bonds rather than having different funds from the same class asset. The mistake some people make is to try to diversify through investing in each fund offered in their 401k.

Maximize Employer's Matching Contribution

To get the most benefits out of your retirement account, employers tend to match the contribution of an employee to a specific ration. It is important for the employee to ensure that they plan their contributions to exploit as much money as the employer avails in a match. This is akin to free money and should not be left to waste.

Aggressive Investment

Invest aggressively, especially if you are a young employee. Remember that a large part of your funding for retirement is coming from Social Security that is basically a low-risk and fixed-return investment. For this reason, you should take significant investment risks with 401k. For instance, invest in growth stocks as well as growth equity portfolio available within your plan. It is important to diversify your investment across different groups of stocks, but invest sensibly.

Non-Revenue Sharing Fund Share

Compared to individual investors, qualified plans that include 401k plans grant employers access to significantly lower cost funds. Investing within the same fund as a person can cost you high fees of what 401k plans can use. It will become a loss to you if your plan is not utilizing them, as you are paying more for the same product due to the fees levies.

Low-Cost Investment

It is recommended that you select a low-cost mutual fund that has a good long-term reputation to invest in, and design a plan as to when to reassign the funds. The reallocation can be on a set basis like twice per year. The mainstream media tends to overplay the shocks in the market, which leads to panic among investors. The timing for making a sale is important to ensure you are in when the market begins to rise again.

Retirement Account and 401k

Consider rolling over your current pensions when tasked with creating a 401k account. The tax agency will take the new 401k into consideration. It is important to engage a professional when doing a rollover and use a trustee rollover. The essence of engaging a professional is to have the money get transferred directly to another provider effectively. The relationship is not documentable by the tax agency and no taxes or penalties are incurred.

Enhance Contributions

Every six months, urge yourself to increase the 401k contributions ratio by say, 1%. For most people, as their incomes grow, their contribution stays stagnant. You should commit to increasing your contribution ratio every six months. Through small increments toward your 401k contributions, you will not feel burdened by the increase.

Critical Success Factors

For one to succeed in a 401k investment, it is important to take into account the time, funds committed, and the selected investment. It is important to balance the consideration of the three pillars identified as the time of investment, funds committed, and the selected investment. You should understand that compounding has a high impact only when handling relatively longer time frames. It is important to commit significantly early enough, say 15% of your income, and if possible, avoid taking loans.

Enhance Your Contributions to Grow Savings

Increase your contributions to grow your retirement savings. People need to make at least 10% savings of their income annually to have a comfortable retirement. However, you can also select the default rate of 8% but have a record kept on ways of how you will increase the savings rate by 1% each year to reach 10-20% of your annual income.

Target Date Fund

Employ target date funds that are easy to apply a solution to, which leaves out the guesswork when optimizing retirement savings investments. A target date funds entail a mixed-assets investment vehicle intended to simplify the need for a defined capital amount by the investor at a future target date like retirement. The structuring of target-date funds is to suitably allocate assets in line with the age and risk level of an investor, as well as automatically scale to the level of risk of assets over a certain period that becomes more conservative as they approach their target date.

Advantages of Using 401k Savings Account

A savings account will enable you to avoid being consumed by the market fluctuations, including the immediate effect it can cause on the 401k. The economy fluctuates because it is complex and will go up and down, but the predicted growth trend is fairly stable. Remember, with the recession, the market will tend to recover and do well over time and you should not make panic decisions.

Plan Advisor

Equally important, you should consider hiring a plan advisor to assist with 401 setups. With a plan advisor, an individual or small business owner will coordinate the 401k plan and invest wisely. Most people might have challenges handling defined contributions plans, due to the comprehensive recordkeeping as well as a selection of investment among other concerns.

Chapter 12: Hang Out with Like-Minded Friends Who are Conscious About their Financial Being

Our circle of friends and social network has a huge impact on our thoughts and approach to life. It is important to gradually surround yourself with friends who share your approach to finances. Remember, if you surround yourself with friends that see no need to draft a personal financial plan, then you are also likely to lack the willpower to resist the denial of comforts induced by following your budget plan. Individuals that share the same view on money and income can help you develop a cohesive approach to financial matters. Another way of creating like-minded friends is to influence your close friends to embrace personal financial planning.

With the advent of social media, you can also exploit the online community to your benefit. For instance,

Personal Finance And Money Management

Facebook offers a group feature where you can pool your like-minded friends or friends with the intention of managing their finances and sharing ideas. Through the sharing of ideas, one benefits from novel ways to manage finances, resources, and feel encouraged that the initiative is noble. With social media, it is important to define rules of engagement and enforce them to ensure the exchange remains beneficial to all the members. For instance, members can share the challenges they are facing with loan repayments, and the other members that are successfully making loan repayments can share their experience for the benefit of all.

For emphasis, the like-minded circle does not mean that you avoid your friends or colleagues. It is important that you furnish those around you who have changed your thinking toward personal finances and believe managing personal finances is important. Then, whenever possible, try to influence the thinking and approach of your friends to personal finances.

Personal Finance And Money Management

The close-knit circle of friends who share your views on personal finances will take shape on its own account. For those friends that do not share your views, make it known to them politely and firmly that you strongly believe in taking the initiative to manage personal finances and invest for the future.

Embracing personal finance management implies that you might have to adjust your lifestyle significantly. For instance, you might reduce or stop frequenting entertainment clubs. Part of your lifestyle adjustment may simply stay at home for a significant part of the weekend to do some online jobs. Friends will try to find out if you are okay and try to win you back to the old life. These friends might go ahead and offer you a soft loan to clear your pending loan and revert you back to your earlier status. For this reason, it is important to be open with your friends that you are okay but have adjusted your life to attain personal finances management.

Personal Finance And Money Management

You should not ignore the potency of peer influence in your life. Friends shape the social life we live to a significant extent. Try to influence a good number of them on the benefits of having a personal financial plan and committing to operationalize it. Remember that not all will buy this idea, while some will take a long time before joining you. The most important for you is to start with a clique of friends who share your views on personal finances to enable the sharing of ideas and encouraging each other.

Conclusion

In conclusion, the reader has been introduced and exposed to what entails personal financial management. The reader has been furnished on how to design personal budget, analyze a potentially good investment, and engage in good debts as opposed to bad debts. The book took time to approach the issue of personal budget on the assumption that the reader is new to the topic and that the reader may have failed before in trying to have a personal financial management plan. For this reason, the author assumed that the reader will fall into the temptation of imposing ideal personal budget goals on himself or herself rather than letting the proposed solution model the wishes of the reader. The author helped guide the reader into financial self-discovery to help generate an intention to manage the finances.

Personal Finance And Money Management

Having put these measures in place, the book discussed ways of saving, ways of generating passive income, and how to turn bad debt into a good debt in the simplest way possible. The reader was taken through the need for diversifying investments and given tips on 401k investments. Understanding that the reader will be motivated to engage in the ideas and strategies suggested, the author introduced the emotive topic of how to detect a scam and avoid scam. Arguably true, scams are among the threats for sustained attempts by individuals to invest. Scammers discourage individuals from trying investments as most people rarely want to risk their hard-earned money again. Overall, this book has comprehensively covered what constitutes personal finance and money management.

Personal Finance And Money Management

Connect with us on our Facebook page

www.facebook.com/bluesourceandfriends and stay tuned to our latest book promotions and free giveaways.

www.ingramcontent.com/pod-product-compliance
Lightning Source LLC
Chambersburg PA
CBHW030726180526
45157CB00008BA/3064